CLEVER
DOG!

CLEVER
DOG!

GWEN BAILEY

Collins

First published in 2009 by
Collins, an imprint of
HarperCollins Publishers
77–85 Fulham Palace Road
Hammersmith, London W6 8JB

The Collins website address is: www.collins.co.uk

Gwen Bailey asserts the moral right to be identified as the author of this work.

A catalogue record for this book is available from the British Library.

Created by: SP Creative Design
Editor: Heather Thomas
Designer: Rolando Ugolini
Photographs: Richard Palmer

ISBN 978-0-00-727993-7

Acknowledgements
The publishers would like to thank the following for their help in producing this book: Anthony Allan and Indie, John Burgoyne and Ollie, Rebecca Cole and Izzie, Mary Felden and Simba, Wendy Grantham and Tom, Steve and Vicky Hailey and Elvis, Susan Hickman and Zania, Steven and Olivia Hill and Molly, Fiona Hutto and Sammy, Claire Luscombe and Sassy, Amanda Menzies and Winston, Sarah Morris and Milly, Daphne Norridge and Obi, Gary and Linda Pickard and Jed, Jill and Immy Pricket and Max, and Jackie and Martin Stuart and Belan.

Colour reproduction by Colourscan, Singapore
Printed and bound in China by Leo Paper

Note: Dogs are referred to as 'he' throughout to avoid 'he'/'she' each time or the rather impersonal 'it'. This reflects no bias towards males, and both sexes are equally valuable and easy to train.

Contents

Introduction   6

Part 1 How to teach your dog anything   8

Part 2 Dog assignments   52
  1 Wet dog dry   56
  2 Back up   58
  3 Go to bed   62
  4 Jump!   66
  5 Take a message   72
  6 Shake!   74
  7 Shut that door!   76
  8 Ring the bell   80
  9 Turn out the light   84
  10 Put toys away   88
  11 Bring my shoes   92
  12 Find lost keys   96
  13 Carry groceries   100
  14 Fetch the phone   104
  15 Bark and quiet   106
  16 Atishoo!   110
  17 Remove socks   114
  18 Pick it up   116
  19 Body search   120
  20 Wave goodbye   124

Index   128

Introduction

Teaching your dog to do something useful is simple when you know how. However, it is not so easy as teaching a human as you have no words to ask for what you want. This book tells you what to do to help your dog understand what you require of him, and how to reward him, so he really wants to do what you ask.

Most dogs love to interact with their owners and they will happily work to please you once they know what to do. Many dogs have a surplus of energy, and tired owners who work for a living often can't keep up with demand for walks and activities. Teaching your dog to be useful around the house is good for both of you. It will not only give you some assistance in your busy life but will also provide your dog with a job and a purpose for living. Creating a relationship where your dog feels loved and valued is really important, and the ideas in this book will help you to achieve that.

Only methods involving positive reinforcement are given throughout. There is no place for force or bullying in dog training. Rewards and encouragement will give you a happy, contented dog who enjoys his work and is willing to do as you ask. Nothing feels as good as successful relationships for members of a social species, and both humans and dogs are highly social. Working in harmony towards a shared goal feels good, and teaching your dog the assignments in this book will bring a sense of achievement and gratification that will be long lasting for both you and your dog. Before long, you will have a willing pair of paws to help you with many jobs around the house.

Part 1
How to teach your dog anything

Teaching dogs to do useful things is fun and remarkably easy when you know how to go about it. In Part 1 of this book you will find all the essential information that you need to know before you begin training your dog to perform the assignments in Part 2.

The desire to work

The many different breeds of dog were created by selective breeding in order to produce animals that were useful for certain types of work.

Dogs with jobs

Dogs were bred to help control vermin, to herd sheep, to work cattle, to hunt game, to retrieve game for hunters and to help fishermen with nets, as well as for a whole range of other tasks that were necessary to help humans prosper. Only a few dogs were kept solely as companions. Most were working dogs that were bred with the energy and stamina to keep them going all day.

The majority of the pedigree dogs we have today are direct descendants of these working breeds and most have

Collies were bred to work and they love to use their considerable mental energy to interact with us and win a favoured treat.

specific hard-wired propensities for a certain behaviour that was useful when they had to work, such as the desire to catch and kill small creatures in dogs used for vermin control, or an insatiable craving to chase in dogs used for herding.

Most dogs are now kept as pets and although they are very good at adapting to new ways, many have the same energy and desire to work that was bred into their ancestors. With busy lives full of work and child care, many owners do not have the time to use up all the mental and physical energy a dog has. This can result in a discontented dog and boisterous, sometimes problematic, behaviour. Giving your dog a job via the assignments in this book can use up all that excess energy as well as giving you a well-trained, useful assistant to help out during everyday life.

When teaching your dog the assignments in this book, you will notice that he learns some more readily than others. This is because different dogs will have different propensities for certain tasks and will find it easier to perform tasks that are similar to the work they have been bred for.

Your dog's genes
Find out what your dog was bred for and what inherited tendencies he has by researching in books and on the internet.

Gundogs

Gundogs are bred to be willing workers, so they try hard and learn readily. They were also bred to be active and they have plenty of stamina, so they will work best and concentrate for longer after being well exercised. Many of the gundogs were developed to retrieve and they readily learn any assignment that involves carrying objects.

Working dogs

Working dogs were bred for a whole range of purposes, so how easily they learn tasks will depend on what they were bred to do. Generally, they are intelligent and learn fast, so they will usually welcome the chance to help you out with daily tasks.

Herding dogs

Dogs bred specifically to herd livestock enjoy running and chasing tasks most of all. They were developed to be very attentive to signals and will learn fast and accurately if you teach them well. Like gundogs, the herding breeds have the stamina to run all day, so always make sure they are well exercised before beginning training.

Terriers

Terriers are bright and alert and will usually learn fast if they can see a reason for doing as you ask. Many breeds were developed to dig and thus they find it easy to do assignments that involve using their paws. However, they are easily excited, and vigorous games incorporated into your training sessions will help move things along faster.

Active and busy, this Spaniel is bred to be a gundog and can easily be taught anything that involves activity, sniffing or fetching.

Hounds

Hounds are often the laziest of dogs in the house, reserving their energies for chasing or running when they are outside. Assignments involving the need to carry objects will be the most taxing for them, but, luckily, many love their food and can become very motivated once they realize it is worth their while performing the required task for an edible reward.

Toys

Dogs bred to be companions are usually willing to please and thrive on affection. Learning tasks was not a requirement for their ancestors and so some can be a little slow to learn. However, all things are possible and, with patience, the smaller toy breeds can develop just as much of a work ethic as those bred for generations to do a job.

What's best for your dog?

Information on the history of dog breeds is easy to come by, so do find out what your dog was bred to do to see what he is likely to be most good at learning. If you have a cross-bred or mix of breeds, look up those most likely to be in his parentage and watch him to see which behaviours he likes to do best. Although all dogs can be taught all assignments, arming yourself with this knowledge will help you to choose the tasks he will find easiest to teach first, and be more patient if he struggles to do those that he is not so well suited for.

The German Shepherd dog is intelligent and eager to please and will really try hard to figure out what he has to do to earn your praise and rewards.

Should dogs work?

Some owners feel it is not appropriate to teach their dogs to do 'chores' and that, because they love them, they should live a life of luxury which caters for their every need. However, for many dogs, this leads to boredom, and they would be more content if they had something to do.

Working leads to fulfilment

Sometimes dogs invent 'jobs' for themselves, such as seeing off people approaching the house, chasing birds out of the garden, or running after joggers or other dogs on a walk. Many behaviour problems start out as a form of energy release for the dog and then develop into bad habits. Knowing that many dogs were bred to work makes it much easier to understand why they feel better and behave more appropriately if given something to do. Channelling their energies and desires for natural behaviour patterns into 'work' of any kind allows positive reward-based chemistry in the brain to make a dog feel good. Asking your dog to do things that are useful to you will make it more likely that you will remember to ask him to do those things rather than teaching party tricks that may get forgotten until the guests arrive. Giving your dog a job will improve the bond between you as well as helping him to feel better about the world and his place in it.

Dogs will soon get bored and lonely if they are not included in their owners' busy lives.

A dog who is happily working will feel contented, useful and valued, compared to a dog who is bored and restless. If you introduce 'jobs' in a positive way and make sure that your dog is well rewarded for his effort, you will find that he really enjoys working for you and both of you will benefit. So teaching your dog to be useful brings advantages for both of you, especially to a canine friend who is ready and willing to be given something to do. And, if you take the trouble to learn how to teach him things, you will find out just how clever he can be!

Keeping your dog active and busy by training him to do enjoyable assignments will use up his excess energy and lead to fulfilment and contentment.

How dogs learn

Knowing how dogs learn is essential if you want to be able to train your dog easily. It may be tempting to skip to the 'assignments' later in this book but studying this section will ensure that training goes smoothly and is more fun.

Trial, error and success!

Dogs learn from trial and error or success – just as we do. Thus they quickly learn which actions will bring pleasant consequences and which are better avoided. For example, a puppy discovers that putting his nose near a hot stove is unpleasant and quickly learns not to do it again. He also finds out that running to his owners when they call him is rewarding because they give him tasty food treats, and thus he learns to do so more often. However, our dogs can also quickly learn things we don't want them to do, such as turning over the bin to find food scraps, or jumping up to get our attention. We need to be aware, all

Dogs learn more quickly if we use rewards to motivate them to do what we want.

the time, of what our dogs are learning and must try to make sure that they are rewarded only for the actions that we want to be repeated.

Positive methods are better

When we train our dogs, it is much better if we use just the positives, rewarding those actions we want to be repeated and ignoring the unwanted ones. This prevents our dogs getting worried about us and avoids any feelings of pressure, concern or avoidance. Using positive methods means that dogs enjoy their training and will learn faster.

When you train using positive methods, make sure that you are always in a positive frame of mind. Being cross, impatient or irritable will make your dog feel bad, too, and will put him off training. Wait until you are feeling happier and your training will progress more quickly.

Asking dogs to do an action with no words

Since our dogs cannot understand English and, consequently, we cannot tell them what we want them to do, we have to find a way of teaching them what we want without using any words. This involves finding a way to get them to perform the required action, which we can reward, and then putting it on cue so they will do it when ever we ask for it.

First, we need to find a suitable way of getting them to do the action we want. The most common method used is luring, whereby a piece of food is used to move the dog into position or get him to perform an action, such as lying down or pawing at something. Discovering a way of using rewards to tempt your dog into trying the required action takes some ingenuity, but, once you have mastered this, anything is possible.

When your dog knows that in the special circumstances that you have created, behaving in a certain way earns him

Advantages of positive training methods

- Kind and not stressful for your dog
- He is in the right frame of mind to learn
- Positive methods are nicer for owners
- The bond between owner/dog grows stronger
- Your dog will not learn to fear owners
- It is easier to undo mistakes
- Your dog will not fear the consequences of making a mistake
- Training is fun for both of you

Training tip

Create a situation where an action occurs, then let your dog know it was right by rewarding him well.

a reward, he will behave in the same way each time. When he is reliably doing the action you want, you can put this on cue by giving the cue just before he does it. If you repeat this many times, your dog will learn to perform the action when you give the cue to get the reward.

Techniques for training actions

• **Luring** This can be done with toys or food rewards. It is useful for encouraging behaviour in 'novice' animals, so that it can be rewarded.

• **Shaping** The dog is rewarded for approximations to the action, e.g. if you want him to stand on a mat, you reward each time he turns towards the mat or moves in that direction. Gradually, the dog moves towards the mat and eventually stands on it. This is useful for 'educated' dogs.

• **Targeting** The dog is taught to touch the target, then the target is held in a position so he has to do the required action to touch it. This is useful for behaviours that are very different to 'natural' behaviours, e.g. turning off a light switch for a disabled person.

• **Mimicry** This usually happens accidentally, e.g. a young, impressionable dog watches and follows an older dog. There is some evidence that dogs can learn by mimicry, but it is not the first choice of most trainers.

• **Modelling** The behaviour is encouraged by moving the animal into

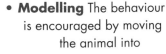

Teaching a dog to touch a target and then moving the target can help achieve behaviours that a dog would not naturally do and which can then be rewarded.

position, e.g. pushing down on the dog's bottom. This is not recommended as the animal resists pressure, thereby taking it longer to learn what is required.

Putting the action on cue

The cue can be a word, sound or signal (see Signals and Words on page 42). The cue needs to be given just before the dog does the action. If you do this repeatedly, eventually leaving a little gap between the cue and whatever you do to make the action happen, your dog will try to work out what you mean. If he has previously learnt that the action results in the reward, he may try the action to see if this is what you want. Reward him well to let him know he has done the right thing. Repeating these learning experiences over time will help him learn to make the connection and he will begin to do the action to get the reward every time you give the cue.

Example of using positive methods

To teach your dog to lie down on cue, first get him into the sit position. The head is then lured downwards by holding a treat just in front of his nose and moving it down slowly (your dog should be able to lick and chew at the treat but cannot get it all). As his head moves down, his neck and shoulders follow and, eventually, it becomes easier for your dog to lie down and then sit in an awkward position. As soon as his elbows hit the floor, the treat is given, together with lots of praise and another treat. He will remember this, and the next time, he will go into the down position more easily. Repeat a few more times and end the session on a success.

In the next session, repeat as above until your dog is going into the down position easily (you should find he is much better at this now than he was during the first session – see latent learning opposite). Make sure you keep all the associations the same, i.e. the

Using food as a lure and then to reward an action gets the dog into position easily and makes him want to do it again. It is a simple and stress-free way to learn tasks.

same place and same position in relation to the dog (see Associations on page 38). Now it is time to add the voice cue and hand signal. Give your cue just ahead of asking for the action (using the food lure) and reward well when the action is offered. Continue to do this for the rest of the session, ending on a success.

In later sessions, you can give your cue, then ask for the required action (using the food lure) and reward the action. Do this several times. Then begin to leave a slightly longer interval between giving the cue and asking for the action to give your dog time to think. During this time, reward any small attempts towards the full action that he may make – just to let him know that he was right to try. As he becomes more proficient, wait for him to perform the full action before rewarding him. If you take this slowly, he will gradually learn to understand your cue. Be patient and always help him out by luring him again if he needs it during later sessions.

Latent learning
When you come back to the same exercise again after taking a break, you will find that your dog seems to respond better. It is almost as if his brain has sorted out the puzzle while it was resting. This could be what is happening or it could be that a rested brain picks things up more easily.

Keep sessions short and fun
Training sessions should only last three minutes as both animals and humans tire easily. End on a good note by stopping when the dog does what is required (rather than trying one last time) or go back to something easy to finish on a positive experience. Always stop if you start feeling frustrated or annoyed as your dog will pick this up and be less willing to work. If training is short, fun and easy, it will happen more often.

Be quiet
Don't say anything during the early part of your dog's training. Vocal humans like to chat, but he will either get distracted and won't be able to concentrate, or will zone you out so that he won't hear you give the voice cue later. Keep quiet and concentrate on getting your actions right in order for your dog to do the right thing.

Superstitious behaviours

These are unnecessary behaviours that a dog learns while he is learning the behaviour you want him to do. They are behaviours that you did not intend him to learn, but he thinks that he has to do them in order to be rewarded. For example, you want your dog to raise one paw to 'wave' and accidentally reward him when he raises two paws (well, he did raise the paw you wanted). From then on, he will try to raise two paws to get the reward. To stop this, go back to the beginning and reward him only when one paw is raised.

In a similar way, dogs may learn to jump or raise a paw when being taught to bark on command.

This dog has learned to bark and raise his left paw at the same time. The owner wanted him to bark on cue, but he thinks he needs to lift his paw as well to get the reward.

Opposite: Don't reward unwanted behaviours with attention or eye contact. Otherwise, they will quickly become a bad habit.

Good relationships

In order to train your dog to do anything, do it willingly, and work in cooperation with you on tasks throughout the day, he has to like you.

Building a relationship

Building a relationship based on love and trust will allow you to reduce reliance on food treats or games and will improve your dog's willingness to please. Anger, impatience and negativity will damage relationships and make him resentful and reluctant. Walking away when you feel yourself getting cross or frustrated will save the relationship.

Good relationships develop over time but being a good consistent leader who encourages and rewards readily will help to speed up the process. Genuine affection given freely and patient teaching will prove that you are trustworthy and will earn your dog's respect and dedication. He will enjoy the affection and effort that comes with the work, and both of you will appreciate the happiness that is engendered by shared experiences and completed tasks. Social bonds formed during working together to solve problems and achieve goals are strong and will feel good for both of you.

A happy and loving relationship is the best place to begin if you want a willing and dedicated partner for your training.

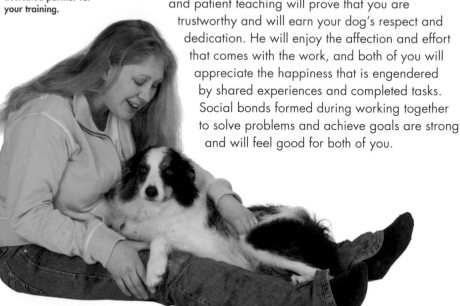

A good relationship focuses your dog's attention on you and he will try hard to please you and do as you ask.

Successful training

If your training sessions are set up carefully and are thought through in advance, the training will go smoothly without hitches, which will be better for both you and your dog.

Aim for success

Try to ensure that you have set up the situation in such a way that your dog does exactly the right thing first time. If it goes wrong, withhold the reward and think about the situation again to ensure success next time. Getting it right first time most of the time will give you painless, error-free learning and prevent frustration and anger/depression on both sides.

The three-minute rule

Train in sessions of three minutes or less. You may be keen to teach your dog something new but learning is tiring and it is important that you give him adequate breaks. Keep lessons short and sweet. Make them fun and plan carefully during the breaks to make the most use of each short lesson. Always end with a success, even if you have to go back to something previously taught. In this way, both of you will look forward to the next session and training will take place as fast as possible.

Is your dog ready to learn?

For a dog to learn easily, he needs to be in the right frame of mind, just as we do. For effective learning, he needs to be:
• Physically well
• Alert and active
• Mentally rested
• Exercised physically but not exhausted
• Unafraid
• Relaxed and happy.

Are you ready to train?

Since your dog cannot learn well without an effective teacher, you also need to be in the right frame of mind to begin the training. You need to be:

- Relaxed and happy
- Not too tired
- Excited about the training
- Unstressed
- In a good mood.

If both you and your dog meet all these conditions, your training session will have the greatest chance of success.

Being consistent with your signals and voice cues will help your dog to learn what is required quickly.

The educated dog

Learning will get faster as your dog becomes more educated, i.e. has had more successful learning experiences. Over time, you will find that it is easier to teach new things to your dog as he will already know the process and will help you by trying to find out what you want so he can get to his rewards more quickly.

Rewards

Food, games with toys and social approval can all be used to motivate and reward your dog when asking him to do things for you. You need to find out what he likes best and then use them individually or in combination.

Rewarding good behaviour

When you first train something new, your dog will need to be rewarded each and every time he gets it right, so that he knows that he has done the task correctly and therefore will repeat the action next time. Don't be mean with the rewards you offer – being generous at the right time will help your dog learn quickly and he is more likely to remain willing to try hard again next time.

Social approval

For most pet dogs, love and affection are not in short supply and they are unlikely to work hard for a long time for this alone. However, social approval is highly rewarding for dogs and showing that you are genuinely pleased with your dog when he gets something right will have a big effect. Affection and approval are important for all dogs but particularly for those that try hard to please and enjoy the closeness of the bond they share with their owner. Some dogs will work hard for their owner's approval alone once they know what to do, but all dogs will learn new tasks more quickly if initially you use food or games as well.

Humans show social approval in two ways – they either vocalize and smile, or they touch, stroke, hug and pat. Check that your dog actually enjoys your attention, particularly if you like to hug or pat. Hands placed roughly on the head, ears and the eye area are often not welcomed by dogs and can have the opposite effect. Instead, praise warmly and touch gently. Genuine pleasure and excitement following a completed task will make a dog more willing to do it again.

Food

Soft, smelly food is usually more appetizing than hard, dry food. Find out what your dog likes best by offering a variety. Food that can be cut into small pieces and won't crumble or flake will be easiest to handle. Try using the following items:

- Cheese
- Sausage
- Meat, especially chicken
- Commercially prepared treats
- Liver (only small amounts).

Praise and attention are very important to dogs, who are social animals like us, particularly if you share a strong bond.

Rewards

Only small pieces are needed as, otherwise, your dog will become too full too quickly. Many small pieces – given individually with praise – are a better reward for holding a position than one large lump swallowed whole.

Be careful to introduce new foods slowly, so that your dog's digestion is not upset. Large amounts of treats are sometimes needed for intensive training days, so build up to these gradually to avoid an upset stomach. Start each training session with enough treats to reward your dog generously and always finish the session before you run out.

Tug games are easy to play with small dogs and provide great enjoyment and reward for those dogs that enjoy them.

Games with toys

If your dog is not particularly interested in food, rewarding him with games with toys is another option. Although it is not as easy to find ways to position the toy to get the desired response as it is when using food, it is still usually possible.

Remember that the dog is usually working for a game with the toy, rather than for just possession of the toy itself, so you will need to spend a few minutes playing with your dog once he has done the right thing. Play whatever game he likes best – choose from chase, tug-of-war, and games with squeaky toys.

Many dogs enjoy the thrill of the chase and capture of toys. Some like the chase, whereas others enjoy possession of the toy once they have caught it.

What does your dog want?

When choosing what to use as a motivator and reward, try to think what your dog would like right now. If you have been using the same food all week, try something different. Dogs get bored with the same treat each time – just as we do – and they may work even harder for something different.

Use food when your dog is not full, but not too hungry either. If he is too full, he will not want the food enough to work hard for it. However, if he is too hungry, he will become obsessed by the food and will find it difficult to concentrate. If your dog is very food-motivated and a little too enthusiastic, you may find it easier to use dry, hard food rather than food that is soft and smelly.

Rewards

Continuous rewards
Always reward your dog each time for complicated tasks, actions that require a lot of effort, or anything that isn't completely learnt or understood. Save random rewards with jackpots for easy tasks that are often repeated.

In a similar way, only try using games as a motivator and reward when your dog is not tired. A long day playing with the children may mean that he is more ready to sleep than work, so choose a time when he is fresh and raring to go.

High-value rewards for difficult tasks

When you have found out what your dog really likes, grade your rewards in order of importance to him (remember that this will vary from time to time as he becomes bored with one thing and starts to prefer another).

You can then use the more favoured rewards for the more difficult tasks or for when he has to work harder to achieve success. Saving these 'special' rewards for such times will mean that your dog will be rewarded well for his extra effort and thus he will make more effort at those times when you need it most. Use the less-favoured food and games for things he knows how to do or tasks that require little effort.

When giving praise, don't pat or stroke your dog's head as he will not like it. Instead, stroke his chest or back.

Random rewards and jackpots

When your dog is learning something new, it is important that he is rewarded every time, so that he knows that he has done something correctly. However, once he has learned a task well, he will work harder and for longer if you begin to gradually reduce the rewards given. At first when you withhold the reward, you will see a look of confusion because he hasn't been rewarded. Praise him to let him know that he was correct and ask for a repeat, then reward the repeat well. Continue in this way, gradually reducing the number of rewards you give until you are rewarding approximately two in every 10 responses at random.

You will find that your dog will begin to gamble on the outcome in a similar way to that in which people gamble on the outcome of a horse race or when playing the lottery and will try hard to 'win' the reward.

You can also raise the performance levels by adding some occasional jackpots for good responses. A jackpot is a whole range of tasty treats or a very special treat, together with lots of praise and games and fun. Really celebrate your dog's 'win'! Giving a jackpot for the best performances will help to motivate him to work really hard to earn them.

A jackpot of rewards is something to be celebrated, like a win on the lottery, and will improve performance and willingness to try.

Timing

The correct timing of the delivery of the reward is very important because you cannot tell your dog what you want him to do in words.

Instant rewards

All you can do is to set up a situation in which your dog is likely to do the right thing and then to reward him instantly when he does so. Rewarding him immediately is like saying to him: 'Well done, that was exactly what I wanted you to do and please do that again next time'.

You have only a second or two to get the reward to your dog after he has performed the required action correctly, but the more instantly the reward appears, the more likely it is that he will make the connection.

If you delay the reward and your dog goes on to thinking about something else or, worse still, does another action, you will be rewarding him for this instead. Rewarding him at this stage is like saying to him: 'Well done, I wanted you to do something other than what I was trying to get you to do in the first

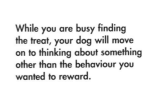

While you are busy finding the treat, your dog will move on to thinking about something other than the behaviour you wanted to reward.

place and please do that again'.
So always have a food treat or toy
ready when you ask for an action.
Don't have it on display or within
scenting range (unless you are
using it as a lure) as that will
distract your dog from the
desired action. Keep it
close by you, or get hold
of it, while your dog is
performing the action,
so you are ready to reward him
as soon as the action is completed.

Using sounds

Some people use a sound to signal
to their dog that he has done the
right thing, and then closely follow
the sound with the reward. Over
time, this sound becomes a signal
of reward, or it can be pre-trained
by pairing the sound with a reward
many times before training begins.
Some people use a click sound
(clicker training) while others
say 'Good boy'. If you are
consistent, this will give
your dog an immediate
indication that he is correct,
and the reward can then be given
to him slightly later.

**While your dog is
still learning what
is required of him,
give him the reward
as soon as he has
done as requested,
so he knows he has
done the correct action.**

Associations

Many people train their dogs at home and they are then disappointed when they will not respond outside or in someone else's home. This is because dogs learn a set of associations rather than just the word or signal that their owners are hoping will be connected to the action they require.

Learning sets of associations

As we cannot tell our dogs or describe what we want them to do, we have to create a situation where they perform the correct action that we then reward and put on cue. The dog then learns all the components that make up that situation, including such things as the following:

- The place you are both in
- Where your dog is in relation to you
- Whether you are standing, sitting, kneeling, leaning forward or standing up straight
- What else is around him
- Whether he is on or off lead.

For example, if you teach a puppy to sit for his dinner in the kitchen while he is standing in front of you and you are holding his dinner dish, he won't understand your cue to 'Sit' when he is standing beside you waiting to cross the road. He isn't being stubborn or stupid; he has learned that 'Sit' means: 'Put your bottom on the ground when you are in the kitchen standing in front of your owner

If you always teach your dog to 'down' when standing, he will learn just this set of associations.

and they are holding your dish saying "Sit" and you will get your dinner'. Take away nearly all of the components that went into making up the situation in which he learned to respond, and he simply does not understand what to do.

Change associations slowly

To overcome this problem, you need to teach your dog, using the same patient procedure, in many different situations, with him in various positions in relation to you and with lots of different things going on around him. Change just one thing at a time, e.g. you may teach him to sit in the garden next to you during one training session and then teach him in the next session to sit in front of you in the garden. In subsequent sessions, however, you may teach him to sit beside you or in front of you in a different environment. Eventually, he will learn to respond to the hand signal or the voice cue by itself and will respond anywhere.

Changing any of the associations before the dog has learned the exercise will cause confusion. Therefore, try to remember, from session to session, where you stood in relation to the dog last time, e.g. whether you were crouching, kneeling, standing, if you were using your left or right hand, etc. If you can keep all the associations the same until your dog has learned the exercise, he will learn more quickly. Then you can change things gradually, one at a time.

Asking him to 'down' when you are squatting rather than standing brings different associations and therefore you may have to help him understand what you mean.

'Sit'
The only cue that most pet dogs understand is 'Sit'. This is because it is taught by owners in a variety of situations and positions and is repeated over and over again until the dog finally understands what the word means.

Expectations

Most training goes wrong because we expect too much of our dogs too soon. Your dog spends most of his time sleeping or just padding around quietly – he doesn't go to school, university or to work all day, using his brain.

Take it slowly

Your dog's brain is relatively unsophisticated in relation to yours and therefore he takes much longer to learn things. Added to that, we can't tell him or describe what we want him to do, so please be patient when training him and make sure you take things slowly and at his speed.

Just because your dog knows how to sit on cue doesn't mean he will understand what you mean if you ask him to sit at a distance.

Be clear about what you want him to do and try to communicate, using signals and gestures as clearly as you can. Repeat the early stages of the exercise during many sessions to give you a firm foundation before moving on. Don't be too impatient to get the end result. Just be happy that you are starting well and get each stage faultless before moving on.

Keep your expectations low

You are not teaching a human child with whom you can communicate easily. You are teaching a member of a different species who does not speak your language. Expecting to go slow will give you a realistic approach and, if you exceed your expectations, you can be proud that your dog is so clever.

Assume lack of understanding

If your dog is not co-operating, assume he doesn't understand what you want, rather than thinking he is being deliberately naughty or stubborn. Make sure he is feeling well and ready to work, that you have a good incentive for him to do as you ask, and try again, going back to basics until he learns what he has to do. Break tasks down into smaller parts and patiently teach every stage until he is completely clear what you want.

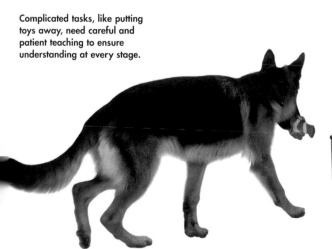

Complicated tasks, like putting toys away, need careful and patient teaching to ensure understanding at every stage.

Signals and words

To communicate with each other, humans have developed a complex speech system with a huge area of their brain devoted to speech recognition and production. However, dogs tend to use body language and scent to communicate.

Body language and scent

Dogs communicate very little with each other by vocalization. Most of their communication with other dogs is via body language and scent, and a large proportion of their brains are dedicated to recognizing movements and smells.

When we train dogs, we are asking them to do something that we know how to do but they do not. The only way we can teach them is to be very clear about what we want. Trying to teach them to learn our words or, worse still, to pick out what we want from a string of sentences as we talk is very difficult.

Using signals and gestures

A better way to approach training is to use a language they understand, involving signals and gestures. When training something new, think hard about what gestures and signals you want to associate with the task. Write these down or draw them, so you use the same ones each time. When you train using these gestures and signals, you will be 'speaking' a different

Try hard to keep your body language signals consistent when training your dog as this will enable him to learn more quickly.

language from the one you usually use, so be very careful what you say. Subtle changes in your gestures and signals will be like saying a word in a different accent. Try to be really clear and consistent with your signals, so that it is easy for your dog to learn them.

Once he has learnt to associate a gesture or signal with a task, teach him to associate a word with this action. To do this, give the word ahead of the gesture or signal to enable him to learn to associate the two things. Given time, and many repetitions, he will begin to understand that the word always precedes the gesture and he will begin to respond with the action you require whenever he hears the word.

Nose licking is a sign of anxiety or conflict. Pressure from the owner to keep still for the photo when this dog wants to run and play results in a quick nose lick to ease tension.

Before you begin

Before you begin training the assignments, it helps to give your dog some basic training, so he is used to learning and you have a number of cues you can give him to settle him and get him into a position where he is ready to learn.

Learning to wait

For all assignments, your dog needs to have learnt to wait for things he wants. If he gets easily frustrated and doesn't know how to deal with these feelings he will be difficult to work with. Ask him to wait for desirable things, such as a favourite toy, his dinner, your attention, or going outside. You don't need to make him wait for long – just a few seconds or a minute until he relaxes. Teaching him to be patient in this way will make it much easier to train the assignments in Part 2 of this book.

Basic training

Before training your dog to perform the assignments in the following pages, he must know how to do the following when he is asked to carry them out:
1 Come when called
2 Lie down when asked
3 Sit when asked.
For some assignments, your dog will also need to know how to do the following:
1 Stay
2 Lie down at a distance
3 Settle down on a blanket or bed and rest.
There are plenty of books available that will teach you how to train your dog effectively, but make sure you choose one that uses only positive training methods with lots of rewards for doing the right thing.

The retrieve

For assignments 10–19, your dog will need to know the retrieve, which is shown on the following pages.

Opposite: Well-socialized dogs are masters of body language and use this to avoid conflict during the important process of scent collection when they are meeting.

The retrieve

No punishing

Never punish your dog for picking up something you don't want him to have. Teach him to retrieve and then praise him for bringing it back to you instead.

Assignments 10–19 all rely on your dog being able to pick something up and then take it somewhere on command. Of course, with a little life experience, all dogs know how to do this without us teaching them, but we need to teach them how to do this when we ask.

Picking up

Before you even begin to teach your dog to bring things to you, encourage him to pick things up. He may find it easiest, at first, to pick up large soft toys.

What to do

1 Throw or move a soft toy erratically in order to get your dog interested. Praise him if he goes near the toy, or touches it with his mouth. As soon as he picks it up, praise him enthusiastically – make that tail wag! Keep trying this,

developing it steadily over many sessions, until he will pick things up and carry them in his mouth. Once he is doing this reliably, use the word 'Fetch!' before you send him towards the object.

2 When he will 'Fetch' – pick up and carry about – soft objects, try moving on to more difficult objects, such as hard ones or with some metal parts, and soft, floppy things that hang down, such as leads or shoe laces. Be patient as it takes time for dogs to learn to carry these things.

3 If he comes to you with the object in his mouth, praise him well and make a big fuss of him, but do not touch the object or try to take it from him. Otherwise, he will learn to avoid you. For now, just let him know what a clever dog he is for holding on to the item.

Training tip

If he avoids you, don't worry as we will tackle that next. Just praise and make a fuss of him from a distance for picking up the object.

Praise is important

This exercise is more difficult if your dog has previously been told off for touching things, but keep trying and he will soon learn that it is now safe to do so.

Bringing back

Once your dog is happy to pick things up, you need to teach him to bring them back to you.

What to do

1 Throw a toy and ask him to 'Fetch!'. As he picks it up, ask him to come to you using your recall command.

2 Run away from him and encourage him to come with you if you need to. If he comes but drops the toy, run to the toy, make it move again and ask him to 'Fetch'.

3 Continue until he comes to you carrying the toy. When he does so, make a big fuss of him but don't touch the toy or his head. Continue to praise him, stroking his body and making a fuss of him until you think he is about to drop the toy.

4 If he has previously learnt to avoid you when he is carrying something, attach a light line to his collar. Ask him to 'Fetch!' as before and, holding the line, call him while walking slowly away. Keep going and use the line to help him to catch up with you. Then stroke his body and give lots of praise and fuss to tell him how clever he is – don't go near his head, so he can feel safe that you won't take the toy.

5 Practise this over several sessions until your dog will happily run to you with whatever he is carrying.

The retrieve

Be gentle

Never lunge forward to grab the toy as your dog will try to avoid you taking it. Ask him to come right up, praise him for doing so and gently take the toy when he is ready to give it up instead.

'Give'

Teaching your dog to give toys directly to your hand saves a lot of bending down and picking them up from the floor.

What to do

1 Ask your dog to 'Fetch!' and call him to you. Praise him well for coming. Wait until he is becoming tired of holding the toy, then produce a tasty treat from your pocket and hold your hand underneath the toy to catch it as it falls. Hold the treat next to your dog's nose and then wait until you see him preparing to let go of the toy so he can take the treat. Say 'Give' and feed the treat as he releases the toy.
2 Practise this over several sessions until your dog will 'give' with the treat out of sight.

Part 2
Dog assignments

Here are 20 interesting and amazing dog assignments to teach your dog, so he can help with your busy life and have lots of fun doing so at the same time. Rewarding him well for doing the correct actions is the key to success.

Golden rules

1 Always keep your training sessions to less than three minutes, and be sure to stop before you or your dog gets tired or cross.

2 Try to end on a success and don't be tempted to ask your dog to repeat the success again in the same session. If success is difficult to achieve, then go back to something you know your dog can do.

3 Don't ever attempt a training session when you or your dog are tired/cross/hungry/frustrated. Always train when both of you are in a good mood.

4 Wait until your dog is a little hungry or playful and really wants to earn a food reward or a game with a toy before you start training.

5 Spread out the training sessions throughout the day to allow for a good rest in between. Several sessions little and often are more conducive to good learning than one mammoth session.

6 During the rest period between sessions, think about what went well, what went wrong, and how you can achieve success during the next session.

7 Break down anything that your dog finds difficult into very small stages.

8 Don't expect your dog to be Einstein. Most of the time, you want him to sit around with his brain in idle mode rather than working at a university level, so try to keep your expectations low.

9 Have patience – you didn't learn how to drive a car, write or even walk in a day and you have a more complex brain than your dog.

10 Try to improve a little every day. It will make the sessions more fun and satisfying for you and your dog.

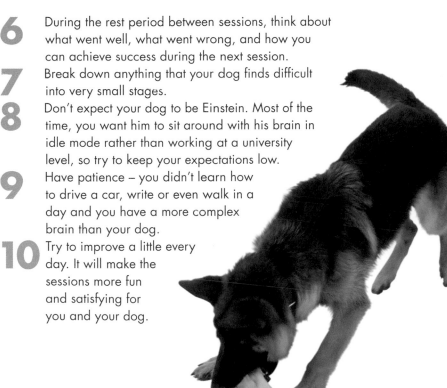

1 Wet dog dry

Pre-training

Your dog needs to feel comfortable with being touched all over and having his paws gently held

Rating

Easy

Equipment

Towel for drying

Even small dogs are difficult to get clean if they don't co-operate. This assignment helps them learn what you need to dry them fast. For large, heavy dogs, this training is a must if you don't want to strain anything as you towel them dry.

Lift your feet

Practise this often with all four feet. Eventually, your dog will begin to shift his weight and lift his foot when you say 'Lift'. Praise him well to let him know how clever he has been.

What to do

1 Choose a leg, ask your dog to 'lift' and tickle gently at the base of the leg, just behind the foot.

2 Keep tickling and drawing his attention to his foot until he shifts his weight onto his other three legs in order that he can move his foot.
3 As soon as he does this, praise him and help him lift his foot, drying it gently with the towel.

Turn around

To save you reaching over, you can teach your dog to turn around when asked.

What to do

1 Call your dog to you and dry the front end with a towel.
2 Say 'Turn around' and lure your dog around with a treat, so he is facing in the opposite direction. Feed the treat and praise him. Hold on to the back end gently, so he cannot spin around to see if you have another treat, and then dry that bit.
3 After many repetitions over successive days, ask your dog to 'Turn around' and delay luring to see if he can work out what to do by himself. Count to 5 before luring him into place. If he moves without the lure, reward him well for being so clever. Keep practising until he really understands what he needs to do.

2 Back up

It's so useful to have a dog that backs up when you ask for those instances when you both get caught in a narrow area with no room to turn around. Here's how to teach your dog.

Pre-training
None

Rating
Easy

Equipment
A sofa pulled away from a wall to form a gap, or a narrow corridor, ideally only just wider than your hips or the dog's (whichever are bigger)

What to do

1 Call your dog to you when you are in the chute, or in a narrow corridor or gap you have constructed for this purpose. Praise him and reward him well with a treat for coming. Ask him to 'Go back' and give your hand signal.

2 Walk slowly towards your dog until you see him move one leg back.

Note: With the 'come when called' and 'back up' cues, you can position your dog exactly where you want him to be in a room – this is useful for directing him to something you would like him to pick up that he just can't seem to find.

3 Stop immediately he moves and reward him well.

Note
If you don't have a 'chute' to begin with, your dog will learn to banana away from you rather than back up straight.

2 Back up

The next stage

• Progress in this way, over several sessions, until your dog is walking backwards as you walk forwards. Remember to give the signal and voice cue in advance of walking forward, and to praise and reward him when he is walking back well (not when he stops or you will be rewarding the stop).

• Once this is very reliable, give your voice cue and signal but do not walk forward. Reward any small movement backwards really well. If, after counting to 5, your dog still hasn't moved, step forward to cause him to move back and then reward the backward movement.

• Build up the backward steps gradually. Begin by rewarding just one, then two, then three etc until he will continue walking back until you reward him (don't let him walk into anything – it is your job to watch where he is going as he is concentrating on you).

What can go wrong?

• If your dog sits, he is confusing your hand signal with the one for 'Sit'. Keep advancing towards him until he jumps up and try again.

• Your dog may twist his bottom round rather than backing up straight because the chute you are training in is too wide. Try a narrower one to start with.

• If your dog stands still rather than going back when you give the signal, he doesn't know the signal yet. Go back to stages 3 and 4.

3 Go to bed

A dog who will 'go to bed' when asked is useful if you are doing something that you don't want him to be involved in. For example, you may be eating or have a visitor who doesn't like dogs.

Pre-training
Down at a distance; settle

Rating
Not quite so easy (harder for energetic dogs)

Equipment
Bed plus toys/treats

What to do
1 Holding your dog's collar in one hand, show him a tasty treat and let him sniff it.

2 Tuck the treat just behind his bed, so it can't be seen but can be found easily. Take your dog a few paces away from the bed, point and say 'Go to bed' before releasing him.

3 Your dog will run to the bed to find the treat. Run to the bed after him and hold him on the bed, praising him well.

4 Ask him to lie down, then reward him for doing so, and stroke him calmly until he is relaxed and has settled down.

3 Go to bed

Progressing the training

- Repeat over many sessions until your dog will run to his bed readily to find the treat from anywhere in the room. Continue to go after him and ask him to lie down and settle so this becomes a habit.
- Hide a treat behind his bed when he is not in the room, bring him in and ask him to 'Go to bed' (don't forget the hand signal). Show him what to do if you need to, and reward him well when he gets there. Ask him to lie down and reward well when he is calm. Repeat until he will always run to his bed when you ask from anywhere in the room.
- Ask him to 'Go to bed' but don't place the treat behind his bed. Let him look for it and when he looks up, throw a treat to land on his bed. Ask him to lie 'Down', running over to him to reward him when he does so (or to help him understand what you mean by 'Down'). Repeat, over several sessions, until he will go to his bed and lie down readily.
- Ask him to go to his bed and when he gets there, ask him to lie down. When he does, throw a treat so it lands close enough to him so he can get it without getting up (get closer if you need; your throws need to be on target). Ask him to 'settle', going over to him soon afterwards to reward him well for doing so. Gradually build this up until you can ask your dog to 'Go to his bed', 'Down' and 'Settle'. Eventually, he will learn the routine and all you will need to say is 'Go to bed' – don't forget to use the accompanying hand signal. Always praise him for

doing so, and make sure that you go and reward him well occasionally for being so clever.

• Practise this in more distracting and exciting circumstances until your dog is reliable about 'going to bed' and settling, whatever else is happening in the room.

Note

Being able to ask your dog to 'go to bed' means that he doesn't have to always be shut away or get shouted at for getting involved when he shouldn't.

What can go wrong

• Keep treats out of the way and ignore your dog completely if he comes to you for them during training. Review your training and try to arrange it so he doesn't make mistakes, allowing you to reward him for the correct behaviour. Placing the pot of treats above his bed where he cannot get them and taking them down from there will help to keep him in place.

• If your dog won't 'go to bed' and stay there when something more exciting is happening, you may be asking for too much too soon. Make sure you have a prompt, accurate response when alone with him first. Gradually increase the distractions and the excitement levels in the room. This is a static exercise and difficult for dogs with lots of energy, so exercise physically and mentally very well first.

4 Jump!

This is very useful for a variety of situations in which your dog may be on the wrong side of an obstruction. If you teach him Stage 7, too, this assignment is useful if an object is on the wrong side of the fence and you can't get over yourself.

Pre-training
None but retrieve for Stage 7 may be useful

Rating
Easy

Equipment
Light-weight line or chord with attachment clip; something adjustable to jump that is not unstable; non-slip surface

What to do
1 On a non-slip surface, begin with a pole on the ground, the sides of the jump in place and holding your dog with a light length of cord clipped to his collar. Tease him with a toy or treat, holding onto his collar.

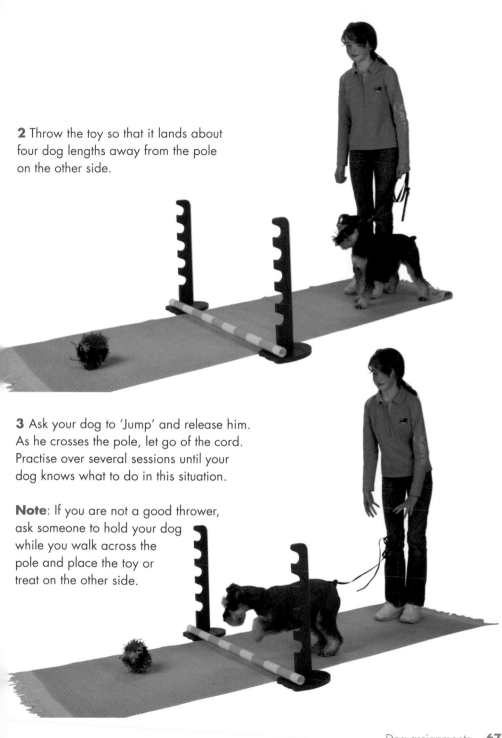

2 Throw the toy so that it lands about four dog lengths away from the pole on the other side.

3 Ask your dog to 'Jump' and release him. As he crosses the pole, let go of the cord. Practise over several sessions until your dog knows what to do in this situation.

Note: If you are not a good thrower, ask someone to hold your dog while you walk across the pole and place the toy or treat on the other side.

4 Jump!

4 Raise the pole by 5cm (2in) and repeat stages 1–3 (see pages 66–67). If your dog tries to go round the jump, rather than over it, use the line to stop him, preferably bringing him to a halt before he gets around the wing. Be prepared to move quickly to the left or right to avoid the tightening cord pulling the jump wings over. Following an unsuccessful attempt, retrieve the toy/treat yourself, leaving your dog in front of the jump (ask someone to hold him if necessary) and try again.

5 Practise this over several sessions until your dog is happy to 'Jump' when you ask him in order to get the toy/treat before raising the height of the jump. Go slowly to allow him to develop his confidence at each height before moving on up.

6 When he will happily jump at all heights, take the jump down to its lowest level and ask him to 'Jump!' without throwing the toy or treat over first. As he jumps, throw the toy/treat so that it lands just in front of him as he lands. Once he is happy with this, you can gradually raise the height again.

7 Once he has learned to jump over, teach him to jump back in the same way, asking someone to hold the cord and use it to stop him coming around the jump if necessary.

4 Jump!

IMPORTANT

Make sure your dog is in good health and is more than 18 months old. Jumping earlier than this can damage growing joints and bones.

8 When he has learned to jump over and back, and he has learned to retrieve, ask him to jump over, pick something up and jump back. You will find that he will drop it as he approaches the jump at first. However, persevere and keep asking and eventually he will jump and carry at the same time. When he does so, reward him well for being so clever.

Dogs love to jump. Taking part in the sport of Agility is a great way for them to have fun and exercise.

What can go wrong

• If your dog doesn't want to jump and he tries everything to avoid doing it, there may be a physical problem for this behaviour. Take him for a full veterinary check and make an appointment with a chiropractor or physiotherapist who specializes in canines.

• If your dog stands and waits when you release him, then try releasing him more quickly after the throw and make it clear that it is OK to move by moving forward yourself and encouraging him forward. Make sure the game with the toy or treat you are using is something your dog really wants.

• A jump falling down may frighten the dog, so that he does not want to jump any more. If this happens, move the jump to a new area and try again. For example, if you were practising in the living room at home, try moving the jump outside to the garden. If necessary, replace the jump with something sturdier if it is likely to happen again.

5 Take a message

Finding someone else in the house is easy for your dog. So why not teach him how to take a message to a named person, so that you don't have to go yourself?

Pre-training
None

Rating
Easy
Especially for a couple, harder for a family

Equipment
Paper and pen

What to do

1 Both people, and your dog, need to be together in the room to start with. If he will hold an item easily, write a note and give it to him to hold. Otherwise, find a way to attach it to his collar. Ask him to 'Go find...' Say the name clearly as this will be important later.

2 The second person calls the dog to them and rewards him well for 'delivering' the note.

3 Repeat, keeping the sender and receiver the same, over several sessions, but varying the place of the receiver in the room, and gradually reducing the calling as your dog gets used to the routine.

4 Repeat Stage 1 but, this time, the receiver needs to leave the room and go just out of sight. Send your dog with a 'Go find...' He may run straight to the receiver, in which case, he should be rewarded well for being so clever. If he doesn't, the receiver should wait until the count of 5 before calling him as before. Repeat the assignment until he will run to the named person immediately.

5 Over several sessions, the receiver needs to get further away, waiting in different rooms and eventually going up or downstairs.

6 Once your dog is reliably going to the named person when sent, and has been doing so for about one month, repeat Stages 1–5 with a different person.

6 Shake!

When dogs shake, the water being held against their body is shaken to the surface where it can be dried easily with a towel.

Why this is useful

Asking your dog to shake before you dry him will remove any excess water. Asking him to shake after you've dried him will allow the rest of the water to come to the surface of the coat so you can remove it.

What to do

Watch your dog carefully when he is very wet, either after a bath or when you bring him home when it has been raining. As he gets ready to shake – he may plant his feet and lift his nose in the air – say 'Shake' and hold out the towel in front of you. Take opportunities when you can to repeat this.

Pre-training
None

Rating
More difficult
Don't expect instant results unless your dog is frequently wet

Equipment needed
A wet dog; a dry towel

Training tip
If your dog is used to learning signals and words, it won't take too many repetitions before he understands what you mean. Gently tickling the ear of a wet dog can sometimes cause him to shake, so try to use this, together with your word and towel signal, at a time when he is very likely to shake in order to get the action on cue.

7 Shut that door!

Pre-training
To target (see page 73)

Rating
A little bit difficult

Equipment
A low cupboard door
that is easy to close;
a pad (or several) of
Post-it notes

Begin training this assignment with some low easy-to-close cupboard doors and then progress later to harder-to-close full-size doors.

What to do
1 Teach your dog to touch his nose on a Post-it note held vertically over several sessions (see page 79).

2 Once he knows how to do this, ask him to 'Push' and wait for him to push his nose into the Post-it before rewarding him. He may not do this at first but be patient and wait for a firm press before rewarding. Gradually build this up until your dog pushes hard on the Post-it every time.

3 For two sessions, hold your hand with the Post-it pad just in front of the open cupboard door at your dog's nose height and ask him to 'Push'. Reward him well.

4 Stick a Post-it note to the door of the cupboard. Put your hand close by and ask him to 'Push'. If he pushes your hand instead of the Post-it, encourage him to push again,

Hand confusion

If your dog tries to target your hand rather than the Post-it note, attach the note to the broad part of a wooden spoon and then try again.

Nose or paw?

Teach your dog to target using his nose first. If you teach the paw touch first (see page 84), he will find it difficult to go back to nosing.

withdrawing your hand at the last minute so the only target he has is the Post-it. Reward him well for touching his nose on the Post-it, and continue to reward correct targeting for several sessions.

5 Once your dog is reliably touching the Post-it note attached to the open cupboard door when you say 'Push', wait for a harder push before rewarding as in Stage 2. Continue, over several sessions, until he will close the cupboard door with his nose when you say 'Push'. Continue to practise until your dog completely understands what you want, and then you can remove the Post-it from the door.

6 Try this exercise on other doors, reverting back to Stage 4 for each new door.

Target training

Target training could not be easier. All you have to do is hold out anything at the level of your dog's nose and then he will approach to sniff it and investigate.

When your dog makes contact with the object, you should reward him well with a tasty food treat. Continue the target training, over several sessions, saying 'Touch' (or, in this case of shutting the door, 'Push') as you present the object.

Eventually, after many patient training sessions, your dog will learn to put his nose on the 'target', wherever it is held or placed, at your command in order to get his reward.

8 Ring the bell

Teaching your dog to ring a bell when he wants to go out can save misunderstandings and toileting accidents. Teaching him to ring a bell when he wants to come in prevents him learning to bark or scratch at the door, which can be a nuisance.

What to do

1 Start the training session by saying 'Bell' and holding out the bell for your dog to sniff.

Pre-training
To target (see page 79)

Rating
Fairly easy

Equipment
A small bell tied to a piece of cord or ribbon

2 Reward your dog enthusiastically when he touches the bell with his nose.

Training tip

Once your dog has learnt this assignment, hang a bell on the outside, too, so he can ring the bell to be let in. Reward him well for doing so and let him know he's really clever.

3 Repeat the assignment over several sessions until he will move towards the bell and touch it with his nose when you say 'Bell'.

4 Tie the bell to the handle of the back door, hold the top of the cord with your hand and say 'Bell'. Reward your dog well when he touches it. Progress until he will touch the bell when you ask without you needing to hold it.

5 Ask him to touch the bell but wait until he has pushed it hard enough to make it ring before rewarding him. Repeat until he pushes the bell hard every time.

Unwanted ringing

Once you have taught this exercise, your dog may begin to ring the bell just to get your attention and some action. See this as a sign that there is not enough going on in his life and give him more exercise – physical and mental. Once he has learnt this exercise really well, only respond to the ringing if you think he has a genuine need to go out.

6 Wait until you think your dog needs to go out. Run to the back door with him, say 'Bell' and let him out as soon as he makes the bell ring. Repeat over several days until he makes the connection between the bell ringing and getting let out. If he goes to the bell and makes it ring at anytime, always be sure to let him out instantly.

9 Turn out the light

Pre-training:

To target – using the paw rather than the nose

Rating:

A little bit difficult

Equipment:

A light switch box (available from a hardware store)

As long as you are not too fussy about paintwork in your house, this is a good exercise to try with bigger dogs. You will need to teach your dog to target with a paw rather than his nose. This is usually easier so any assignments that need the nose should be taught first to avoid confusion.

What to do

1 Teach your dog to target a light switch box using a paw over several sessions and reward well (see page 87).

2 Hold the light switch box underneath the real light switch at about the height your dog's paw will reach naturally if he lifts it forwards. Ask him to 'Press' and reward any attempt to do so, even if it is not perfect at first. Continue at this height over several sessions until you get a perfect response each time.

3 Gradually raise the height of the light switch box on the wall over several sessions. Your dog may find it quite difficult once the box goes about head height and you may need to encourage him to run at the wall, so that he has enough momentum to reach up with his paw. Continue at each height until he can do it easily before moving on.

4 When you reach the height of the light switch, hold the light switch box over it, but remove it at the last second, so

your dog's paw rests on the real light switch. Reward well. Continue to do this until you no longer need the box to show him what to do and he will rest his paw on the real light switch when you say 'Press'. Reward all presses at first until your dog can do this well. Then wait for harder presses before rewarding until, eventually, he paws hard enough to switch off the light. Praise and reward really well and celebrate with your dog because he was so clever!

Target training using a paw
If you have already trained your dog to target using his nose, this training assignment will be quite difficult for him at first as he learns to do something different in response to a similar set of associations.

1 Start with presenting the target on the flat of your hand on the floor next to your dog's paw. If you have previously trained him to nose the target, this is what he will probably do. Withhold rewards and praise, and encourage him to try again. Keep trying until, in frustration, he moves his paw.

2 Reward instantly, even if your dog didn't touch the target, and try again. If he finds this really difficult, then press gently against the side of his paw so he moves it. Reward any small movements of the paw at first and ask for touches later. Keep working at this until he understands that he needs to touch the target with his paw.

3 Then begin to say 'Press' just before you present the target. Over several sessions, work on this until he will readily touch the target with his paw when you say 'Press'. Continue until he will 'press' a target held vertically with his paw.

Right or left?

Dogs are either left-pawed or right-pawed. Knowing which paw your dog favours will help you to make it easier for him to do as you ask.

10 Put toys away

Dogs find it really easy to make a mess, so teach them to tidy up afterwards by putting rubbish into the bin or their toys into the toy box. This is easy to teach, but it's difficult for them to learn, so lots of patience and rewards are essential.

Pre-training
Retrieve (see page 46)

Rating
Not too difficult but lots of patience required

Equipment needed
A rubbish bin or toy box with a large opening; easy-to-pick-up 'rubbish' items or toys

What to do

1 Ask your dog to 'Fetch!' an item and then call him to you. Lure him towards the top of the toy box or bin with your hands.

2 As he approaches, wait until his head is over the opening and say 'Drop', pointing with your finger into the box and dropping the treat into it (initially, you may need to lean the bin a little towards his head).

3 Repeat until he is readily coming forward and putting his head into the box to find his treat. If he drops the toy before he gets to the box, enthusiastically ask him to 'Fetch!' again and repeat, thinking about and changing what you do to make it easier for him to get it right. Continue, over several sessions, until he is readily coming to the box to drop his toy to retrieve his treat.

4 For the next few sessions, ask him to come to the box, point with your finger and say 'Drop!', but do not drop the treat in this time.

Teaching two things

One of the reasons this is difficult is that you are asking your dog to do two things – hold the object and put his head over the box. When dogs learn a second thing (putting head into/over the box), they usually forget to do the first (holding the object). You must patiently repeat this until your dog understands what to do.

5 As soon as he drops the toy, feed the treat and give lots of praise. Repeat until he is readily coming forward with the toy and dropping it in the box.

6 Keep encouraging him to pick up the toy when he drops it in the wrong place until he understands what is needed. Over several sessions, he will start making a conscious effort to drop the object into the box, collecting it when it falls short. Repeat as before, but lean back so your finger is not pointing directly at the box. Help him to get it right if necessary.

7 Gradually, as he learns more, move further from the box until you can get him to pick up items, drop them into the box, and then come to you for the treat. Continue in this way until he knows exactly what to do. Reward him well when he gets it right and let him know he is really clever.

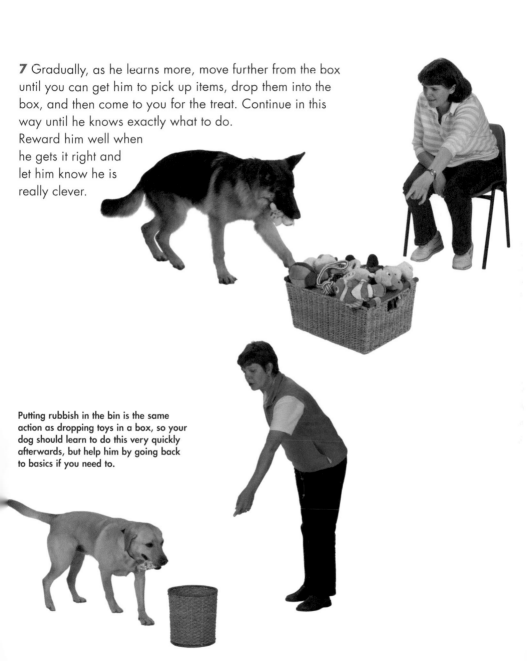

Putting rubbish in the bin is the same action as dropping toys in a box, so your dog should learn to do this very quickly afterwards, but help him by going back to basics if you need to.

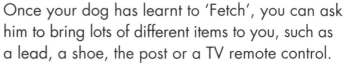

11 Bring my shoes

Once your dog has learnt to 'Fetch', you can ask him to bring lots of different items to you, such as a lead, a shoe, the post or a TV remote control.

Pre-training
Retrieve (see page 46)

Rating
Easy once you have the retrieve

Equipment
Objects to 'Fetch', e.g. a shoe

What to do
1 Choose an easy object to start with, such as a shoe. Clear away anything else that your dog is likely to pick up and then place the shoe in the middle of the floor. Say 'Shoe' and give your hand signal if you are using one (see page 95), then say 'Fetch'.

2 Repeat over several training sessions until your dog will fetch the shoe as soon as you say 'Shoe'. Repetition is the secret. The more you do this, the easier he will find it to learn the word. Spread out many very short sessions over successive days to avoid your dog becoming bored and make sure that the rewards are good.

Training tip

Teaching the names of objects is tricky at first because dogs find it difficult to learn words, but it gets easier as they become 'educated' and you add more words to their repertoire.

3 Repeat stage 1 with another object, e.g. a slipper, practising until your dog really knows the name of this object. Put the shoe and the slipper on the floor and ask him for the 'Shoe'. He will probably bring the slipper as you have been practising this most recently. If he does, accept it quietly with no praise and ask him for the 'Shoe'. Go crazy when he brings the shoe and tell him how clever he is. Repeat this exercise until he is reliably bringing the shoe, then, during the next session, ask for the 'Slipper'. Continue, working over several weeks, until he knows what each sound means.

Other objects

Teach your dog the names of other objects in a similar way. Once he knows the name of an object, move everything out of the way and hide the object just out of sight. Ask him for the object and let him find it. Gradually extend this until he will bring you the object from another room or anywhere in the house. Reward him really well for being so clever.

Using hand signals

Dogs find it much easier to learn hand signals than words, so to make it simpler for your dog, think up a unique hand signal for each object and show that as you say the word.

Bringing the post when it is put through the letterbox can be taught easily once your dog has learnt how to pick up flat letters off the carpet and carry big packets.

Teaching your dog to bring his lead should be really easy if you take him for a walk once he has done so.

12 Find lost keys

Pre-training
Retrieve (see page 46)

Rating
A little difficult

Equipment
Old bunch of keys
attached to a large,
soft key-ring

Imagine that you have just walked through a field with your dog and you get back to the car to discover that you've lost your keys on the way. Searching for them with your eyes will take a long time. However, your dog, when trained, will be able to find them much more quickly and easily by searching with his nose.

What to do

1 Begin teaching your dog this assignment with several training sessions of throwing the keys just in front of him.

2 Ask your dog to 'Fetch' and send him to collect the keys.

3 Give your dog lots of rewards and lavish praise for bringing the keys back to you and continue practising this until he does it easily.

4 The next step is to move from a hard surface to grass. Throw the keys in the same way so they fall in the long grass. Ask your dog to 'Find' and send him off to look for them. Repeat over several sessions, gradually increasing the distance, so that he has to use his nose in order to find them. Eventually cover his eyes as you throw them, so he does not know where they are and has to search for them.

5 On a playing field with short grass, put the keys down when your dog isn't looking and walk on a few paces. Ask him to 'Find' and praise him well when he does so and returns the keys to you. Gradually build this up until you can walk a long distance from the keys and can send your dog to find them.

Training tip
Always mark the
position of the keys
carefully as you place
them by noting two
landmarks at 90
degrees to each other,
so you can help your
dog search in the right
place if he is struggling
to find them.

13 Carry groceries

Rating

Easy once you have
the retrieve

Equipment

A range of items for your
dog to carry, e.g.
cardboard boxes, small
plastic water bottles, etc.

Asking your dog to carry something for you
when you bring in the shopping can be useful
to you as well as helping to give him a sense
of purpose and keeping him active and happy.

What to do

1 Begin with an object that is
easy to carry, fairly small and
lightweight – until your dog is
accomplished, it may be better
to use a weighted cardboard
box or a filled plastic bottle,
so you don't have to worry
if it is destroyed during
training. Offer him the
item and ask him to 'Hold'.

2 If he doesn't take it, tease him with it, then roll it along the floor and ask him to 'Fetch'. Repeat over several sessions until he will 'hold' the item when you pass it to him. Remember to praise him well and tell him how clever he is.

3 Once he will hold items easily, give him an item to hold and walk away from him slowly, encouraging him to follow. If he drops it, ask him to 'Fetch' and move away again. Praise him for walking with you, carrying the item, and tell him how clever he is.

4 Teach your dog to carry various items in different areas, so you can make use of his new talent around the house and garden. Gradually teach him to carry things that are heavier or a little more difficult to hold.

Training tip

At first, your dog will only be able to carry the items for relatively short distances before giving up and putting the object down. Try to gauge when he is close to giving up, then ask him to give it to you and reward him really well with a tasty treat and lots of praise.

Gradually, start asking him to carry things a little further. It will really help to praise him enthusiastically and tell him how clever he is being while he does it. Eventually, he will be able to carry items all the way from the car to the kitchen and will patiently wait until you have put your bags down before bringing the item to you.

14 Fetch the phone

Pre-training

Retrieve (see page 46)
and 'Bring my shoes'
(see page 92)

Rating

Easy if you have already
worked on Assignment
10 (see page 88)

Equipment

An old phone to
practise with

If you are constantly losing your handset or
mobile phone, or you are busy in another room,
this assignment is not only very useful for you
but it can be fun for your dog, too.

What to do

1 Begin by practising retrieves with an old handset or mobile
phone. Make it fun and reward your dog well when he picks
it up. Reward him again when he brings it to you. If he finds
it difficult to pick up the phone, wrap a piece of cloth tightly
around it so he can get a grip. Keep working with him until
he can pick it up easily.

2 Place the phone in different locations and ask him to bring
it to you. Work with this until he will retrieve it and knows
what you mean when you ask for the 'Phone'.

3 Place the phone on a low table at his nose height and
ask him to retrieve it.

4 Substitute your real phone for the old one. Repeat
until he will bring it to you from wherever it is.

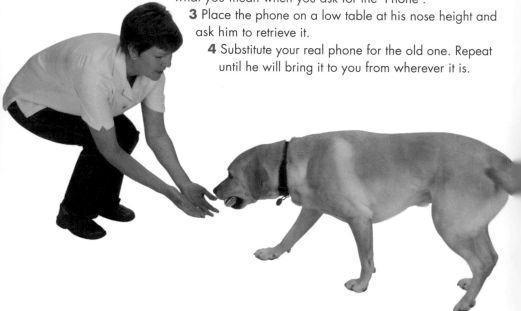

5 Turn the ringer volume on the phone down as low as it will go and arrange for someone to call you. Ask him to fetch the phone while it is ringing, encouraging him if necessary and being close to receive it so he doesn't have to carry it very far at first. Reward him well. Gradually develop this until he will happily retrieve the ringing phone from anywhere in the house. Remember to reward him well while you answer.

No vibrations

If you are using a mobile, turn the vibration function off while you train as this may put your dog off. Once he is happy to bring the phone when it is ringing, re-train from the beginning with the vibration function on.

15 Bark and quiet

Having a dog who will 'bark' on command is useful if you find yourself in need of protection. To teach this assignment effectively, you must choose a time when your dog has plenty of energy and find something he really wants.

'Bark'

What to do

1 Attach your dog's lead and loop the handle over something secure. Stand just out of reach and tease him with a treat or toy, putting lots of energy into this, moving around and making him really want to be where you are. Eventually, in frustration, he will whine or make some noise. Reward instantly!

2 Repeat over many sessions, rewarding whines, squeaks and small noises at first and gradually progressing by waiting to reward only small barks, then loud barks, and finally a series of barks. As soon as your dog is reliably barking, ask for this behaviour with the voice cue 'Bark', together with a hand signal, just before you begin to tease.

3 Progress gradually until your dog will start barking when you ask and keep barking until you throw the treat or toy.

Pre-training
None

Rating
Difficult

Equipment
Motivators; lead; an assistant for the final stages

'Quiet'

What to do
1 Ask your dog to 'bark' and wait until he does. Say 'Quiet' and give a hand signal. Wait for him to stop barking and reward instantly. Repeat several times during a short session.
2 Over a series of short sessions, sometimes reward him for barking and at other times reward him for quiet, having given him extremely clear voice cues and hand signals each time. Gradually, he will learn what 'quiet' means and will stop barking as soon as he sees and hears the signal.
3 Begin to extend the period of quiet. Count to 1 and then reward him, then 2 and reward, and so on. Don't forget to reward the barking often. If you ask for quiet, and, while you are counting, he begins to bark again, ignore it and wait for quiet before rewarding. If this happens, it is a sign that you are moving too fast, so go back to rewarding more quickly and progress more slowly.

Tip
Teaching a 'quiet' is essential to prevent excessive noise that could disturb your neighbours.

Before trying this part of the assignment, make sure your dog will bark on command when he is in any position in relation to you, not just when he is standing facing you (see Associations page 38)

Bark at someone

In the previous stages, your dog was looking towards you while barking. The following stages will teach him to bark at someone while he is beside you. This is useful if you need protection, but be careful how you use it as being barked at by a dog can be frightening. He is only barking because he wants his reward – but the person doesn't know that.

What to do

1 Ask your assistant to stand in front of you, tease your dog with his toy, then hold it behind her back.

2 Ask your dog to 'Bark'. Instruct your assistant to wait for one bark and then to immediately throw him the reward. Praise him well. Repeat over several sessions until your dog understands what to do, then ask him to 'Bark' during the next session without being shown the toy by the assistant. They should throw him the toy after one bark and you should praise him as before.

Visitors

Practise at the front door with your assistant standing outside. This could be very useful one day if you have an unwelcome visitor. Make sure the barking is under your control and you can stop it with a 'quiet' easily.

16 Atishoo!

Bringing you a tissue when you sneeze is not only useful but impressive (unless you have a dog that drools excessively). Combine this with Assignment 9 (see page 84) and you won't have to leave the sofa if you have a cold!

Pre-training
Retrieve (see page 46)

Rating
Reasonably easy

Equipment
Several boxes of tissues

What to do
1 Play retrieve games with a tissue over several sessions, so your dog gets used to delivering it to you and the feel of the paper in his mouth.
2 Place the tissue box on the floor with a tissue removed and lightly tucked back into the box so your dog can lift it easily. Ask him to 'Fetch!' and reward him well for bringing it to you.

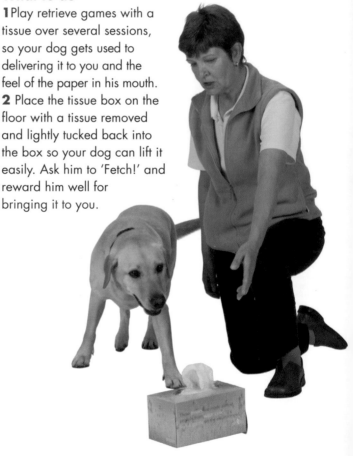

3 During the next session, set up the tissue as in Stage 2, then give a convincing fake sneeze and ask your dog to 'Fetch'.

4 Repeat over several sessions until your dog runs to fetch the tissue as soon as you sneeze. Make sure you reward him well for being so clever.

Progressing the training

Using a full box

Later you can teach your dog how to pull the tissues out of a full box, so you don't have to keep on loosening them for him. He needs to learn to pull them slowly and vertically, so the box doesn't fall over. Put the box back on the floor while you help him learn this. You can weight the bottom of the box to make it easier for him to do this initially.

5 Put the tissues on a low table. Depending on how vigorous your dog is, stick the box to the table at first to prevent it sliding off as he takes the tissue. Give a fake sneeze.

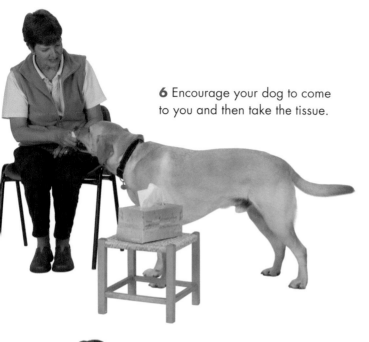

6 Encourage your dog to come to you and then take the tissue.

Training tip

Teach your dog to find the tissue box in different places. Once he will look for, find and bring you a tissue when you sneeze, begin to combine it with putting the tissue in the bin afterwards. Reward him well at every stage and let him know how clever he is.

7 Reward your dog well with treats and plenty of praise.

17 Remove socks

This is an easy assignment for dogs who love to tug and is useful for people who find it difficult to reach their feet. Expect your footwear not to last long if you do this or buy extremely strong socks!

Pre-training
None

Rating
Easy

Equipment
Old socks

What to do
1 Hold the top of the sock and wriggle it in front of your dog until he tries to grab it. Hold it up so he can only reach the toe and praise him when he takes it. Pull a little on the sock, so he pulls back, and encourage him when he does this.

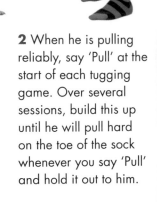

2 When he is pulling reliably, say 'Pull' at the start of each tugging game. Over several sessions, build this up until he will pull hard on the toe of the sock whenever you say 'Pull' and hold it out to him.

3 Ask him to wait (or ask someone to hold him) while you put your foot in the top of the leg part of the sock, leaving some of the leg part and foot of the sock dangling. Ask him to 'Pull' and wriggle your foot to make the spare piece of sock dangle alluringly. Praise him for tugging and reward him with lots of excited praise when he removes the sock from your foot.

Take care!

Teaching this assignment to young dogs may encourage them to chase feet or nip at toes. Be careful to keep control and provide plenty of energy release in exuberant games that don't involve feet.

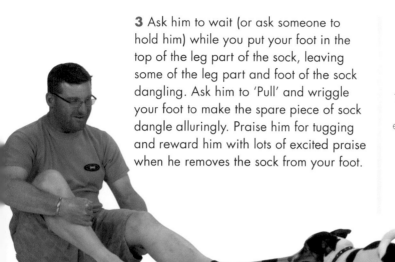

4 Over several sessions, gradually increase the amount of foot you put into the sock until he will help you pull off socks that are almost on. Reward him well for being so clever.

18 Pick it up

A dog who will pick up whatever objects you drop is really useful to have around the house, especially if you have trouble bending down.

Pre-training

Retrieve (see page 46)

Rating

Easy

Equipment

Objects to 'accidentally' drop

What to do

1 Choose an object that your dog is used to retrieving. Play a few retrieve games before you start the training session.

2 Stand up, walk away and drop the object. It is likely that your dog will pick it up. Watch him over your shoulder and, if he does, go wild with enthusiasm and praise. Ask him to bring it to you and reward him. If he doesn't, call 'fetch!' over your shoulder and praise and reward well. If there is still no result, turn and face him, ask him to 'fetch' and reward well. Repeat often over several sessions until he will pick up the object that you have dropped as you walk away while your back is turned.

3 During the next session, watch him carefully to check he has picked up the object but keep on walking. If he picks it up and waits, uncertain what to do, call him to you, praising him when he does. If he comes to you, encourage him to come around to the front of you, so you can reward him and take the object.

Continue practising this over several sessions until your dog is picking up the object and coming round in front of you with it. Make sure that you reward him well.

4 Repeat stages 1 and 2 with different objects in different locations.

19 Body search

Pre-training

Sit; a strong desire to play with toys

Rating

Quite difficult

Equipment

A flat toy; unused tea bags or similar; a flat toy into which the tea bags can be inserted; loose-fitting clothes; assistants for the later stages

This is the fun version of sniffer dog training. Sniffing out hidden substances is easy for your dog – you just have to put it on cue. Begin with searching for his toys and move on to teaching him to search for smaller things, e.g. a tea bag.

What to do

1 Begin by playing an exciting game with a flat toy.

2 Hide it inside your jacket, then do it up and encourage your dog to find it by sniffing.

3 As soon as he has located the toy under your jacket, tell him how clever he is, and ask him to sit. When he sits, remove the toy and throw it to him. Repeat over several sessions, hiding it in different places on your body until he can sniff it out easily and always sits when he finds it. Put a name to this task, such as 'Search'.

4 Get an assistant to hide the toy about their person. Ask your dog to 'Search' and let him use his nose to find it.

5 Encourage him to sit when he finds the toy and reward him with lots of praise and a game with an identical toy. Continue over several sessions until he will find the toy hidden on your assistant in different places.

Impressive scenting
Although quite difficult to teach, this task is easy for dogs with their keen sense of smell and looks impressive to humans who sense mainly with their eyes. Make sure all the humans taking part do so willingly and without being pressured.

6 Introduce another assistant, hiding the toy on one of them, and then ask him to 'Search'. Encourage him to sit when he finds it and reward him well as before.

7 Place tea bags or similar strong smelling substances inside a flat toy. Make this your dog's only toy for a few weeks until he readily searches it out and plays with it. Once he knows the smell and gets excited at the thought of a game with it, repeat stage 1.

8 Repeat stages 2 and 3, hiding only the tea bags rather than the toy. Keep the toy to reward him with when he gets it right. Work on this over many sessions, gradually reducing the quantity of tea until he can find just one bag hidden in someone's clothes.

20 Wave goodbye

This is particularly useful if you have a large, scary-looking dog and want to put shy children or adults at ease. A dog who is sitting and waving at them is unlikely to attack them and usually causes enough smiles to break the ice.

Pre-training

None, although target training using a paw is useful (see page 87)

Rating

Reasonably easy

Equipment

None necessary

What to do

1 Wrap a treat in your hand so your dog can smell it but cannot eat it. Move it about a little to keep his interest and wait until he scrapes at your hand with his paw. Open your hand instantly to feed the treat and give lots of praise. If it doesn't seem as though he will move his paw, press gently against the side of his foot so that he does. Reward instantly and ask for a little more next time. Keep going over several sessions until he will readily touch your hand at ground level as soon as you put it close to his paw.

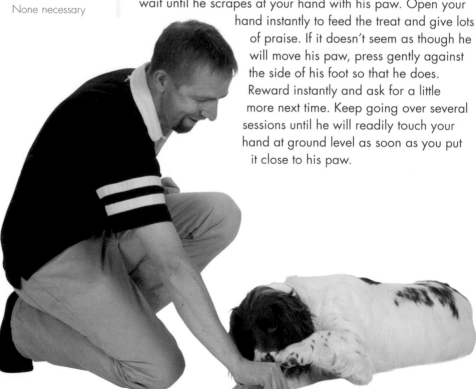

A light touch

If your dog scrapes hard at your hand with his paw, get quicker at opening your hand to feed the treat. If you do this, he will learn that he only needs to use the lightest of touches to get his reward.

2 For the next session, after two or three successful touches, lift your hand about 5cm (2in) off the ground. Wait for him to touch your hand and instantly reward him enthusiastically. Over several sessions, raise the height of your hand until it is level with his head.

Goodbye

Although this task isn't really useful, you can use it to make people feel at ease with your dog or to show children you mean no harm. Waving goodbye to guests makes for a memorable exit.

3 For the next session, after two or three successful touches at head height, present your hand about 5cm (2in) above his head. Wait for him to try to touch your hand with his paw. This is difficult, so be patient. If he is finding it really difficult, lower your hand again and do a successful head-height touch before trying again. Reward any raising of the paw, even to a low height, instantly. Over several sessions, slowly raise your hand until he will raise his paw when he sees your curled hand at waist level. Over several more sessions, develop your curled hand signal into a wave signal and put a voice cue in front of it.

4 When your dog understands your voice cue and hand signal, begin to withhold rewards until he tries extra hard with a higher wave in the air. Praise him, reward him and tell him he is really clever!

Index

associations 22–23, 38–39
atishoo 110–113
back up 58–61
bad habits 14
barking 106, 108–109
basic training 45
behaviour problems 14
body language 42
body search 120–123
bring my shoes 92–95
carry groceries 100–103
carrying objects 13, 100–103
chasing 13
clicker training 37
cross-breeds 13
cues 20, 21, 22
fetch the phone 104–105
find lost keys 96–99
food rewards 31–32, 33
games 32, 34, 54
go to bed 62–65
gundogs 11, 12
hand signals 23, 95
herding dogs 10, 11, 12
hounds 13
jackpots 34–35
jumping 66–71
latent learning 22, 23
learning 16–25, 28, 38–39, 54
luring 20, 23
mimicry 20
modelling 20–21
pedigree dogs 10
pick it up 116–119
positive training methods 19, 22–23
positive reinforcement 6
punishment 46, 64

put toys away 88–91
quiet 107
random rewards 34–35
relationship building 26
remove socks 114–115
retrieve 11, 46–51, 70, 88–91, 92–95,
    96–99, 100–103, 104–105,
    110–113, 116–119
rewards 15, 19, 21, 30–35, 36–37, 54
ring the bell 80–83
scent 42, 123
selective breeding 10
shake 74–75
shaping 20
shut the door 76–79
signals 21, 42–43
'Sit' 39
social approval 30
social bonds 26
sounds 37
superstitious behaviours 24
take a message 72–73
target training 76–79, 84–87
targeting 20, 76–79, 84–87
three-minute rule 28
timing 36–37
toy dogs 13
toys 32, 54, 88–91, 120
training sessions 23, 28–29, 54, 55
turn out the light 84–87
vermin control 10, 11
visitors 109
vocalization 42
wave goodbye 124–127
wet dog dry 56–57
words 42–43
working dogs 10, 11